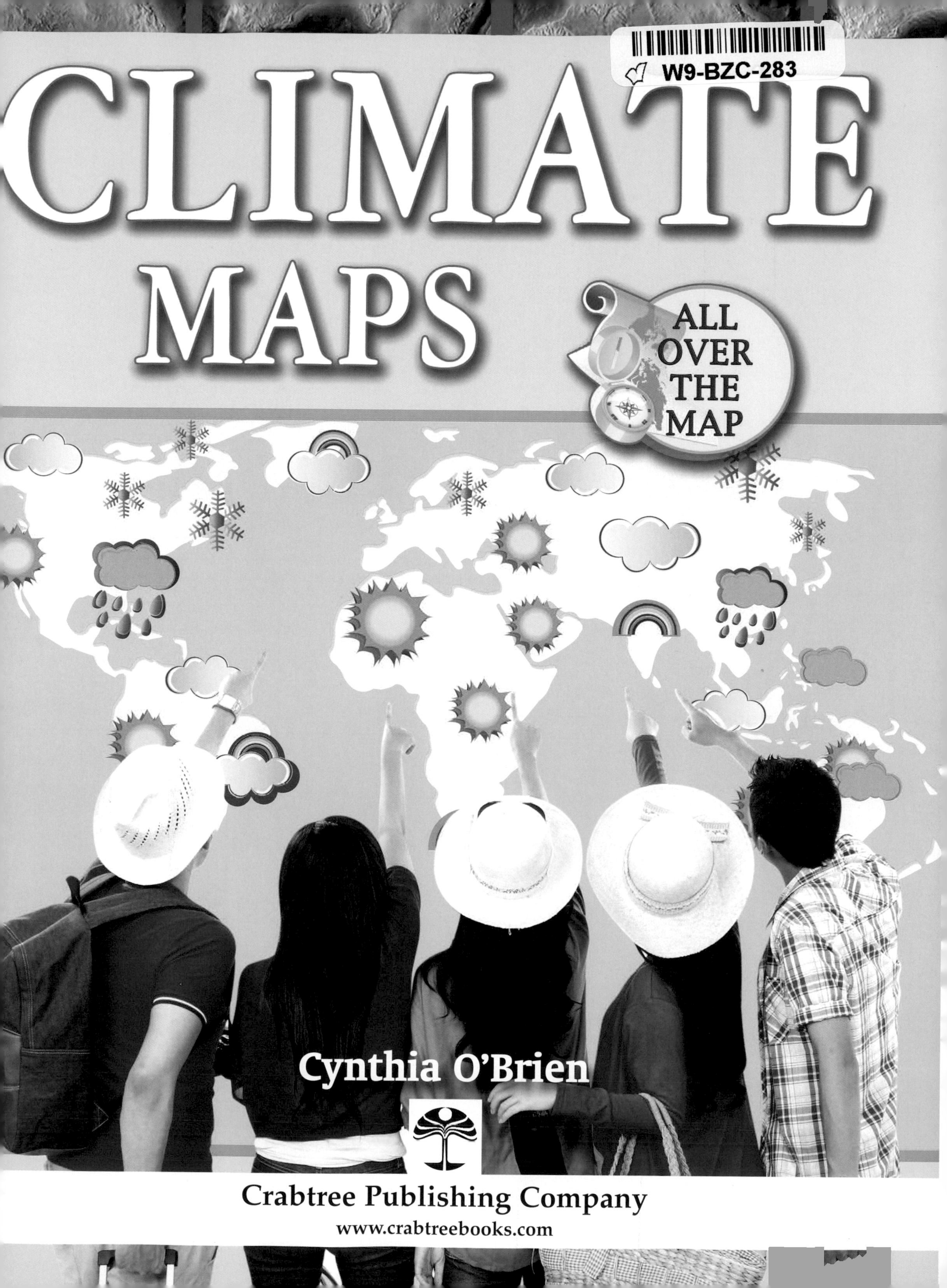
W9-BZC-283
CLIMATE MAPS
ALL OVER THE MAP
Cynthia O'Brien
Crabtree Publishing Company
www.crabtreebooks.com

Crabtree Publishing Company

www.crabtreebooks.com

Author: Cynthia O'Brien
Publishing plan research and development:
Sean Charlebois, Reagan Miller
Crabtree Publishing Company
Series editor: Valerie J. Weber
Editors: Valerie J. Weber, Kelly McNiven, Reagan Miller
Proofreaders: Sangeeta Gupta, Crystal Sikkens, Jessica Shapiro
Editorial director: Kathy Middleton
Project manager: Summit Kumar (Q2A Bill Smith)
Art direction: Joita Das (Q2A Bill Smith)
Design: Roshan (Q2A Bill Smith)
Cover design: Ken Wright
Photo research: Ranjana Batra (Q2A Bill Smith)
Production coordinator and prepress technician: Katherine Berti
Print coordinators: Katherine Berti, Margaret Amy Salter

Photographs:
Cover: olkapooh/Shutterstock (cl); Cover: Digital Vision (tl, br, bl); P1: Nuiiko/Shutterstock (t); P1: Odua Images/Shutterstock (b); P4: djgis/Shutterstock; P6: Dmytro Pylypenko/Shutterstock(tl); P6: SF photo/Shutterstock(bl); P7: apdesign/Shutterstock(tl); P7: steba/ Shutterstock(tr); P7: Pakhnyushcha/Shutterstock(cr); P7: irisphoto1/ Shutterstock(br); P9: Galyna Andrushko /Shutterstock; P11: colacat /Shutterstock; P12: STEPHEN KRASEMANN/SCIENCE PHOTO LIBRARY; P14: Patrick Foto/Shutterstock; P19: Wollertz/Shutterstock; P21: Nuno Miguel Lopes/Shutterstock; P22-23: NASA/JPL; P23: nvelichko/ Shutterstock(t); P25: Alfie Photography/Shutterstock; P26-27: NASA; P27:Luba V Nel/Shutterstock; P29: Christopher Wood/Shutterstock; P30: Monkey Business Images/Shutterstock; P31: Monkey Business Images/Shutterstock

Q2A Art Bank: Pages 5, 6-7, 8, 9, 10, 13, 15, 16, 17, 18, 20, 24-25, 28

t=top, tr=top right, tl=top left, bl= bottom left, br=bottom right, b=bottom, cl=center left

Library and Archives Canada Cataloguing in Publication

O'Brien, Cynthia Jane
Climate maps / Cynthia O'Brien.

(All over the map)
Includes index.
Issued also in electronic format.
ISBN 978-0-7787-4491-7 (bound).--ISBN 978-0-7787-4496-2 (pbk.)

1. Climatology--Maps--Juvenile literature. 2. Map reading--Juvenile literature. I. Title. II. Series: All over the map (St. Catharines, Ont.)

G1046.C8O27 2013 j551.6022'3 C2012-908543-X

Library of Congress Cataloging-in-Publication Data

O'Brien, Cynthia J.
Climate maps / Cynthia O'Brien.
pages cm. -- (All over the map)
Includes index.
ISBN 978-0-7787-4491-7 (reinforced library binding) -- ISBN 978-0-7787-4496-2 (pbk.) -- ISBN 978-1-4271-9329-2 (electronic pdf.) -- ISBN 978-1-4271-9317-9 (electronic html.)
1. Maps--Juvenile literature. 2. Weather--Maps--Juvenile literature. I. Title.

GA105.6.O27 2013
551.6022'3--dc23

2012049907

Printed in Canada/102017/MQ20170731

Crabtree Publishing Company
www.crabtreebooks.com 1-800-387-7650

Copyright © **2013 CRABTREE PUBLISHING COMPANY**. All rights reserved. No part of this publication may be reproduced, stored in a retrieval system or be transmitted in any form or by any means, electronic, mechanical, photocopying, recording, or otherwise, without the prior written permission of Crabtree Publishing Company. In Canada: We acknowledge the financial support of the Government of Canada through the Canada Book Fund for our publishing activities.

Published in Canada
Crabtree Publishing
616 Welland Ave.
St. Catharines, ON
L2M 5V6

Published in the United States
Crabtree Publishing
PMB 59051
350 Fifth Avenue, 59th Floor
New York, New York 10118

Published in the United Kingdom
Crabtree Publishing
Maritime House
Basin Road North, Hove
BN41 1WR

Published in Australia
Crabtree Publishing
3 Charles Street
Coburg North
VIC, 3058

CONTENTS

What is a Climate Map?

Maps give us important information about the world. **Political maps** show countries and cities. **Physical maps** show features such as mountains, rivers, and lakes. A **climate map** can tell you about different weather patterns in a country, or even the whole world.

This hiker is using a physical map to help her find her way. What other kinds of maps might she use to plan her trip?

Climate is the **average** weather in an area over a long period of time. Climate includes the **temperature**, or how hot or cold a place is, and **precipitation**, such as rain or snow, of an area. Weather changes from day to day. For example, one day could be sunny and the next could be raining. Climate, however, is the weather people expect in a certain place at a certain time of year.

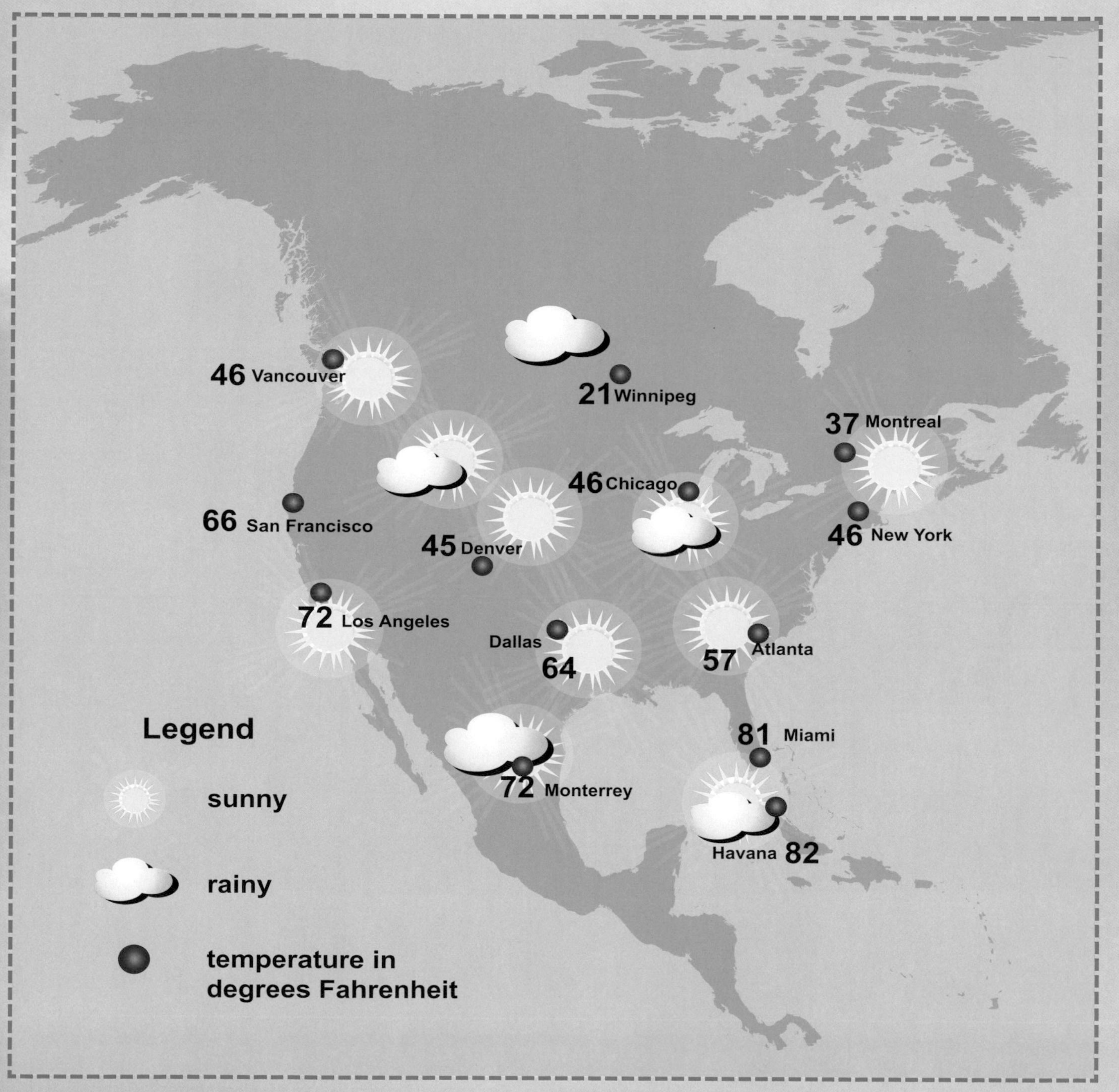

Weather maps, like the one shown here, use ***symbols*** *to show us whether a place will be sunny or rainy on a particular day. They also show us the temperature.*

World Climate Zones

A world climate map is divided into **climate zones**, or areas that share similar climate features such as temperature and rainfall. These zones on the map are identified using different colors. The **legend** shows which color represents each climate. Look at the map below. The same climate can be found in many different parts of the world.

polar

The pictures around the map show different climates.

temperate

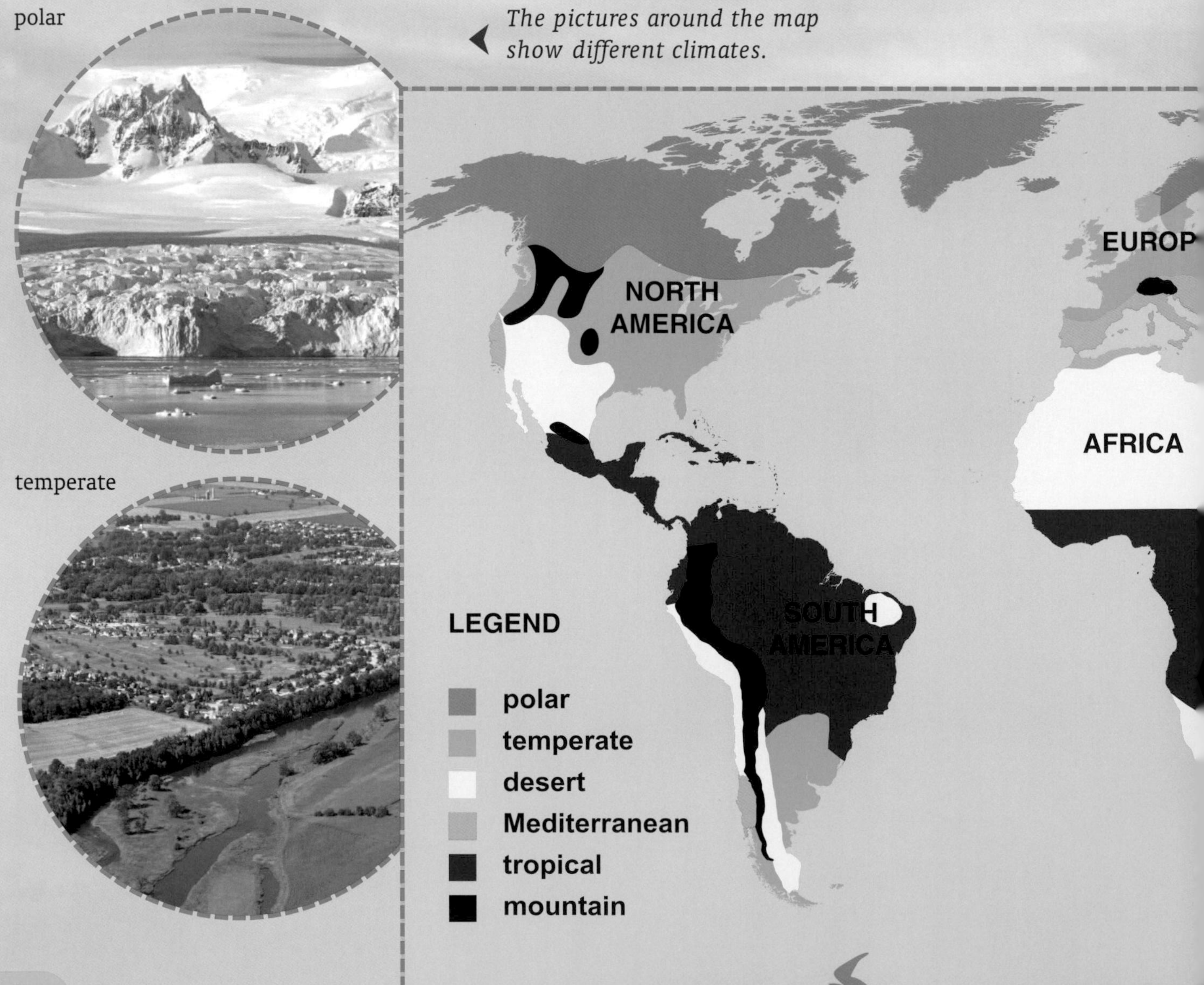

A polar climate, in places like Alaska, is dry and cold. Most of North America has a temperate climate with cold winters and mild summers. A desert climate is dry and hot. A Mediterranean climate has mild winters and hot, dry summers. Italy has a Mediterranean climate. Tropical climate zones are hot and wet, like Hawaii. A mountain climate is wet and windy. Which climate zone would be your first choice to live in? Why?

desert

Mediterranean

tropical

CLIMATE ZONES OF THE WORLD

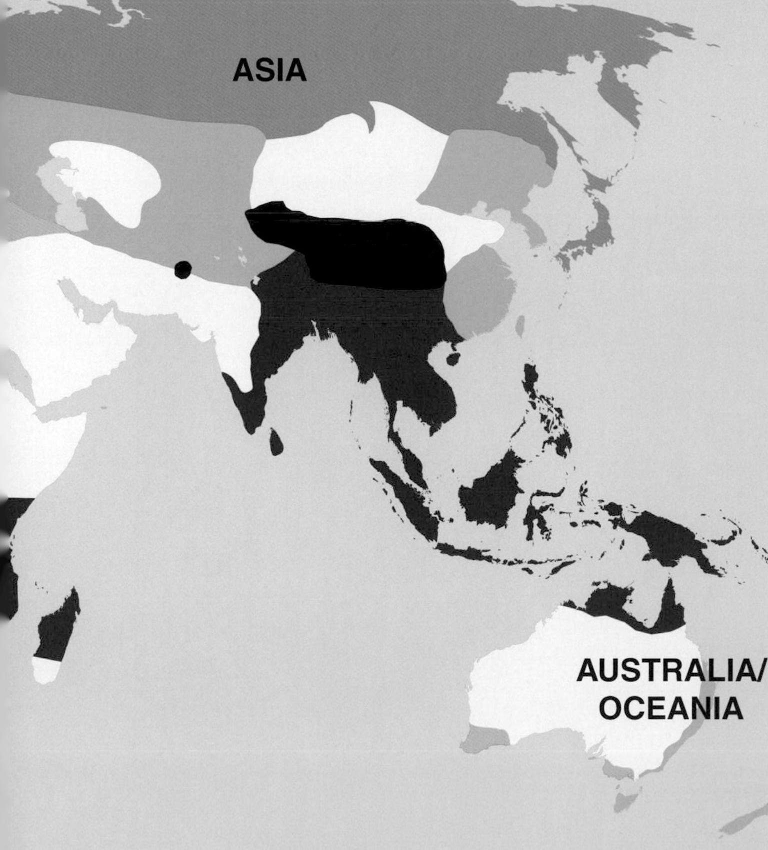

mountain

Latitude and Climate

The type of climate a place has depends on where it is located in the world. Lines of latitude are **horizontal** imaginary lines that are used to measure how far a place is from the **equator**. The equator is a line at the center of Earth that divides the world into two parts: the Northern Hemisphere and the Southern Hemisphere. The latitude of a place affects how warm it is. Areas near the equator are the warmest. Areas further from the equator are colder.

Look at the map below. Which climate zones are the warmest? Which climate zone is the coldest?

Run your finger along a latitude line. Look at the climates around the line. Are they the same or different?

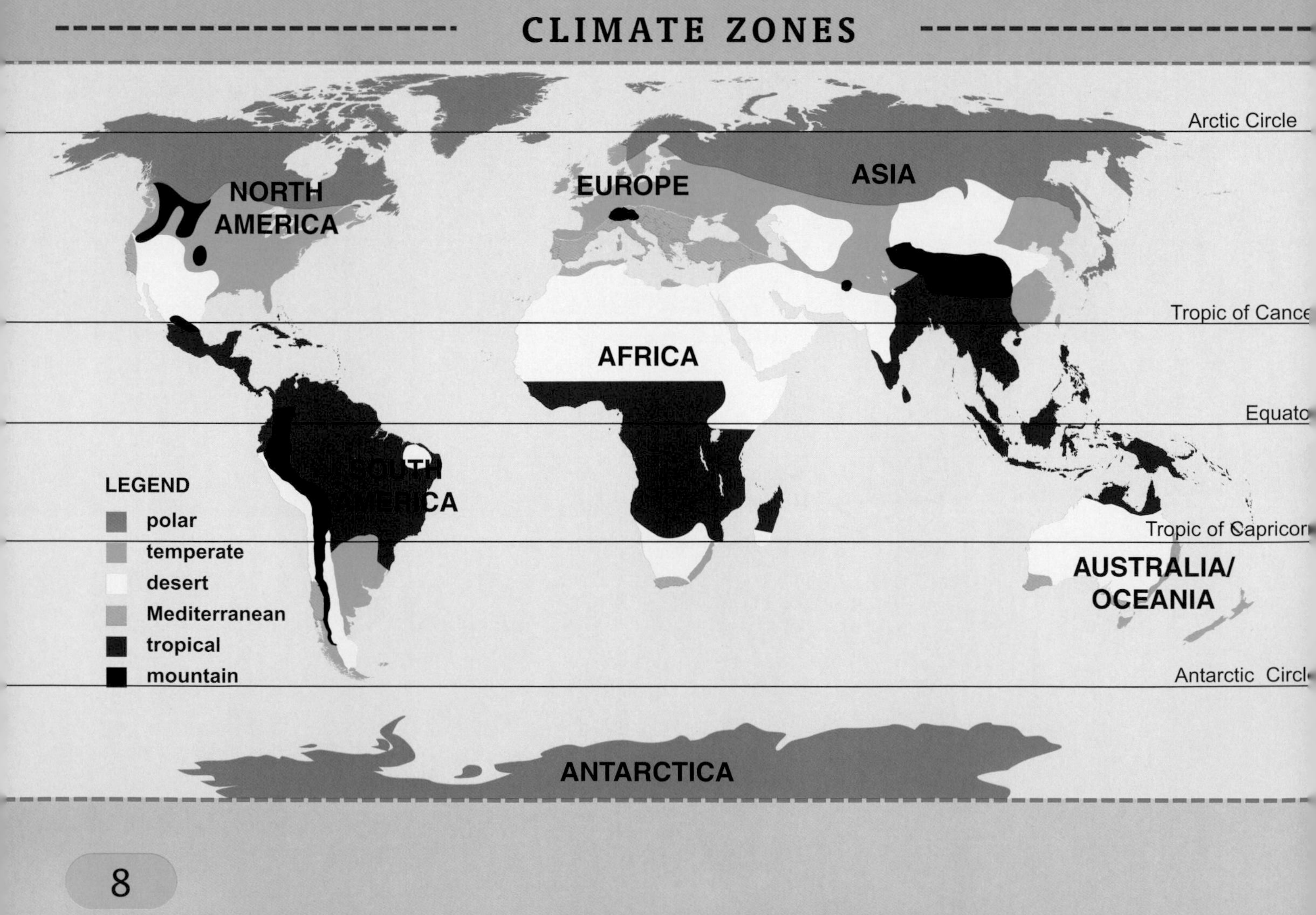

At the equator, the hours of sunlight and darkness are the same. There are 12 hours of daylight and 12 hours of darkness.

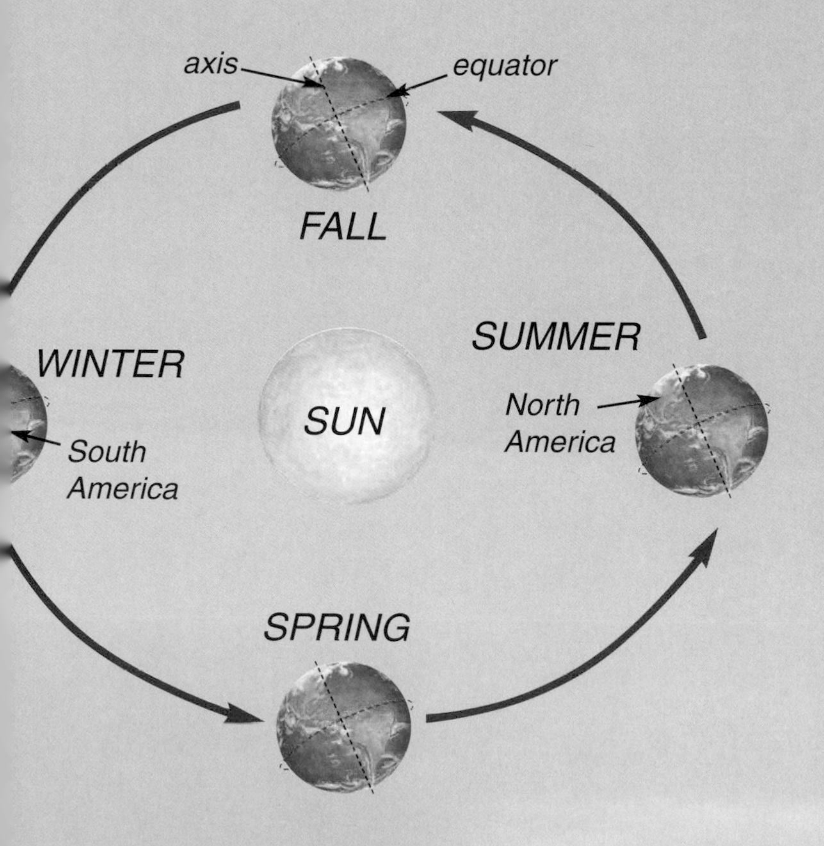

The amount of sunlight an area receives affects its climate. Earth turns on its **axis** once each day, which gives us day and night. Earth travels around the Sun once each year. The Earth's axis is tilted. This means that as the Earth travels around the Sun, the amount of sunlight changes for different parts of the world during different times of the year. Climate zones near the equator have about the same amount of sunlight all year so they have the hottest temperatures.

Small Climate Zones

Did you know that your backyard has its own climate? It is called a **microclimate**. Microclimates occur in small areas. The weather can be different in a small place compared to what is around it. Some microclimates are larger than others. This map of Hawaii shows four climate zones. However, if we could zoom in, we would find even more microclimates.

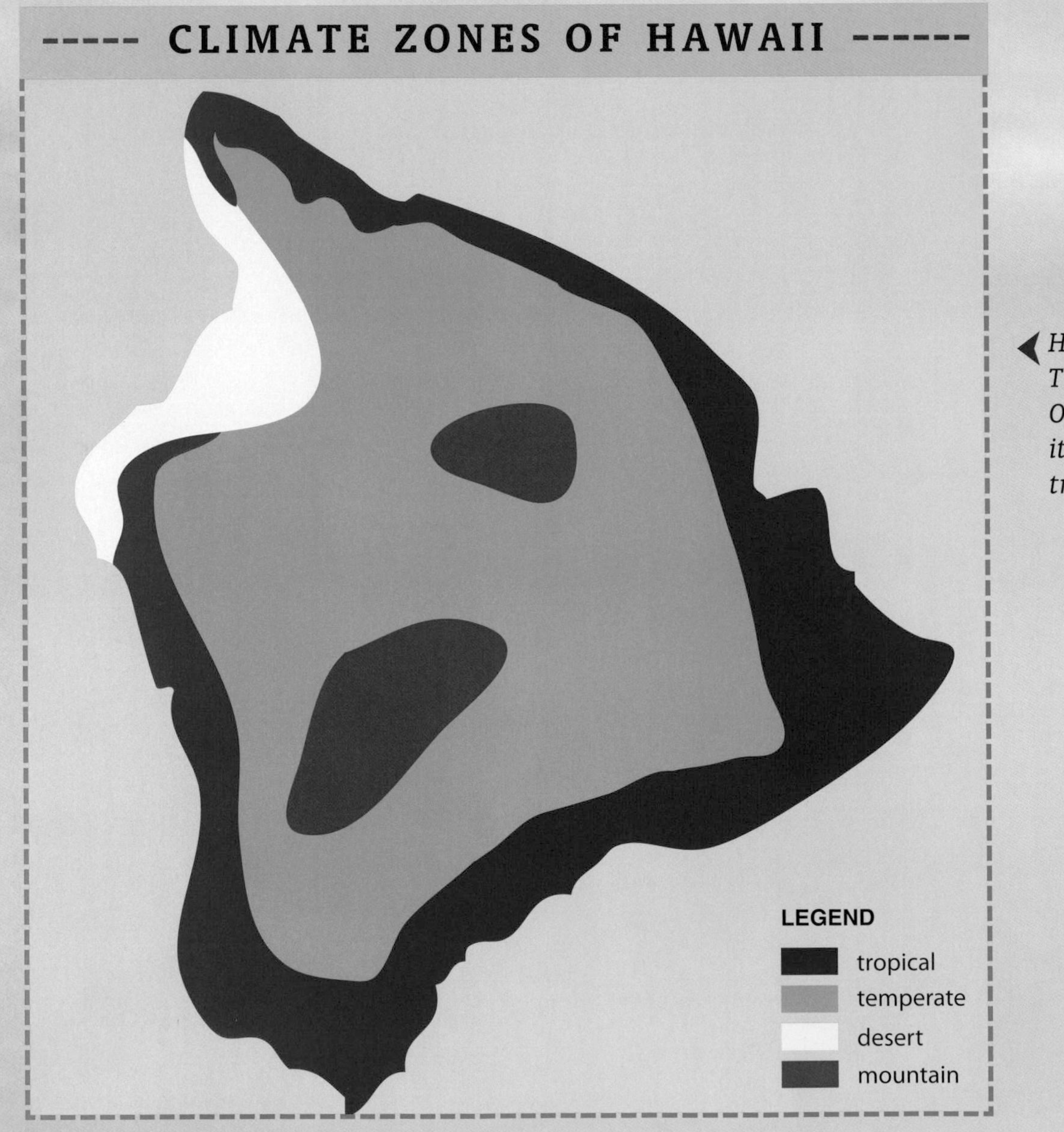

Hawaii is an island. The warm Pacific Ocean is all around it. Where are its tropical zones?

A city is an example of a microclimate. Tall buildings block the wind and the rain. In the summer, the Sun heats up the concrete buildings and sidewalks. The hot concrete warms the air making the temperature increase. This process makes cities warmer than towns nearby.

Learning about microclimates can help gardeners and farmers know what kind of plants or **crops** will grow best in their area. This way a farmer can plant the crops that need a lot of sunlight in the fields that get the most Sun.

These ridges in Peru are used to create microclimates to research how different crops might grow at different heights.

Collecting Data

Climatologists are scientists who study climate. They use tools to measure and record different parts of the weather, such as temperature and precipitation. In some areas, **weather stations** are built to help scientists study patterns in the weather. A weather station can record information over a long period of time to help find out the average weather.

Climatologists read the data off of a weather station.

Climatologists show the results of their research on climate charts and graphs, like the one shown below. The results of a climatologist's research help **cartographers**, or mapmakers, create climate maps. Today, most maps are made using computer programs.

Map Facts

A climate map usually shows one type of weather condition. Precipitation maps and temperature maps are two of the most common types of climate maps. The title of a climate map shows the information represented on the map.

Miami, FL, USA

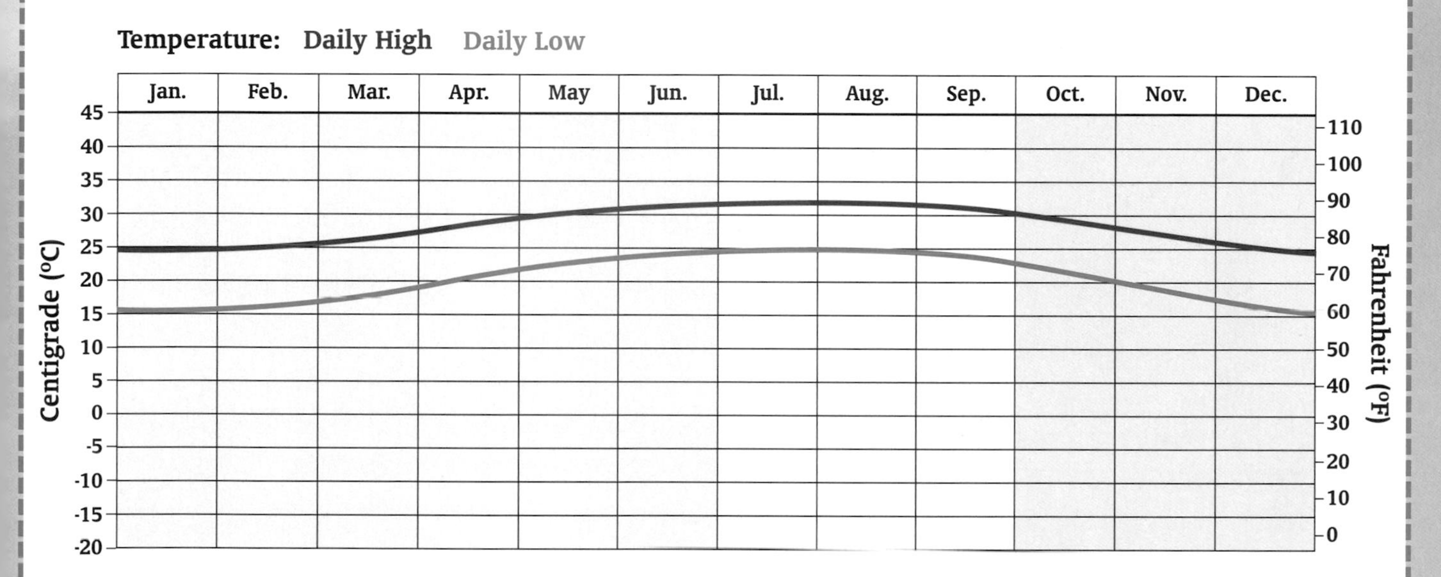

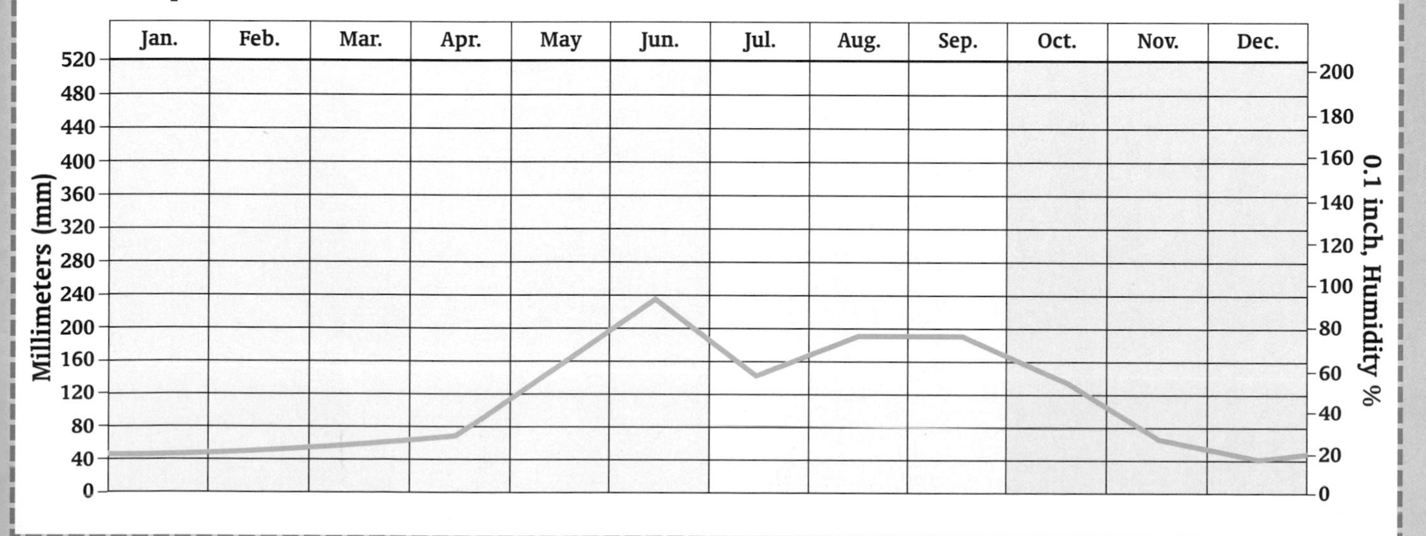

Using Climate Maps

Climate maps tell us a lot about places. Climate maps are very useful to gardeners. Some types of plants grow best in specific climates. A climate map can help a gardener plan which plants will grow best in the climate where he or she lives.

Certain plants, like the rambutan plant shown below, grow best in a tropical climate zone. Would this plant grow where you live?

CLIMATE ZONES OF THE UNITED STATES

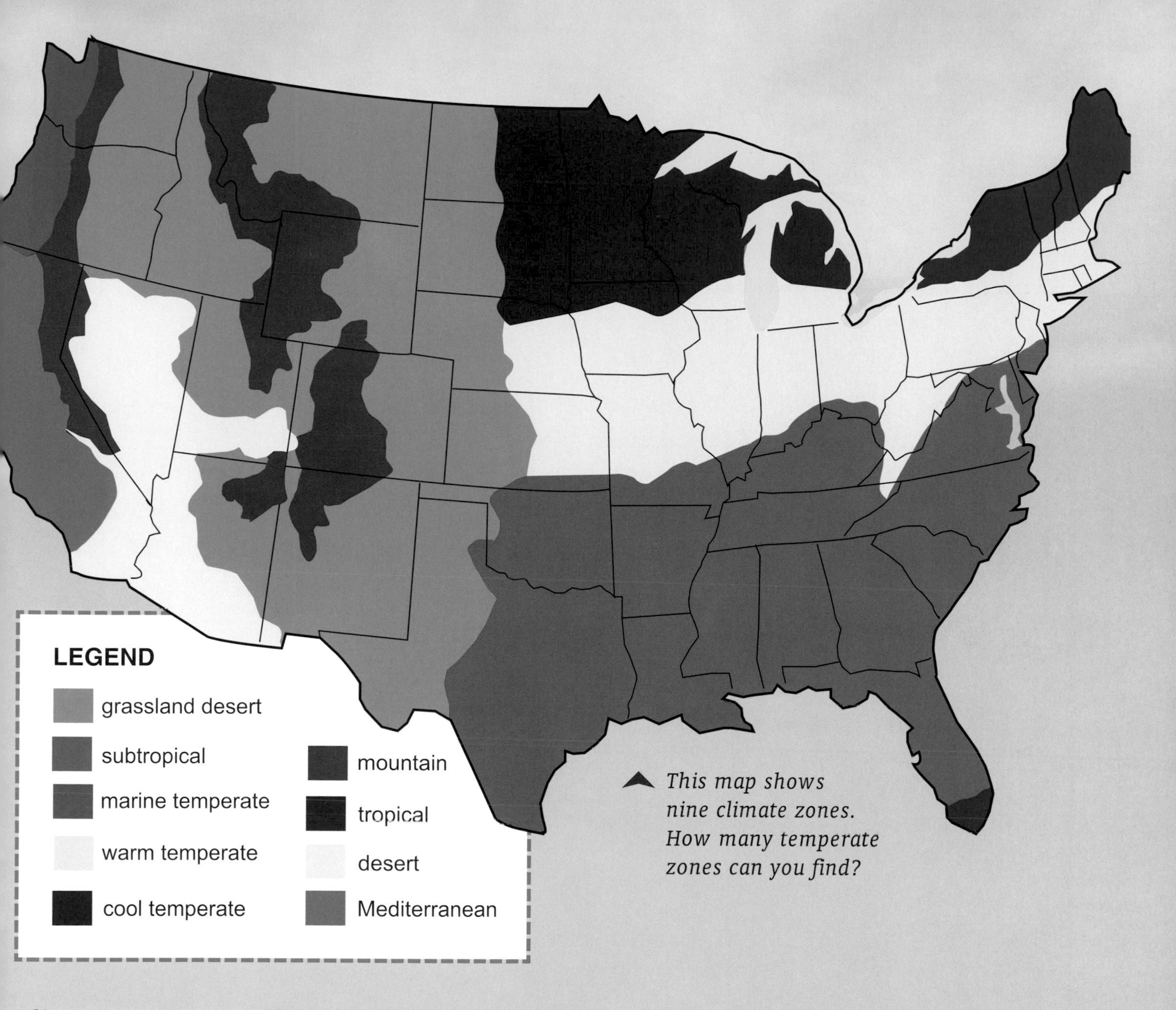

This map shows nine climate zones. How many temperate zones can you find?

Climate maps are also helpful when planning a trip. This map shows the different climate zones in the United States. You could not see the U.S. tropical zone on the big world map. Can you spot it on this map?

Can you see the orange part of the map? Why would this be a good spot to travel for a vacation at the beach? What color are the mountain areas? What would the climate be like there?

Temperature Maps

Temperatures change day to day. Climate is based on average temperatures over a period of time. Look at the maps on these two pages. One map shows us the average temperatures in North America in January. The other map shows us the average temperatures in July. When we look at both of them, we can compare the change of temperature anywhere in North America.

Map Facts

On a temperature map, colors are used to show different temperatures. Colors like red, orange, and yellow usually represent warmer temperatures. Green, blue, or purple often stand for cooler temperatures.

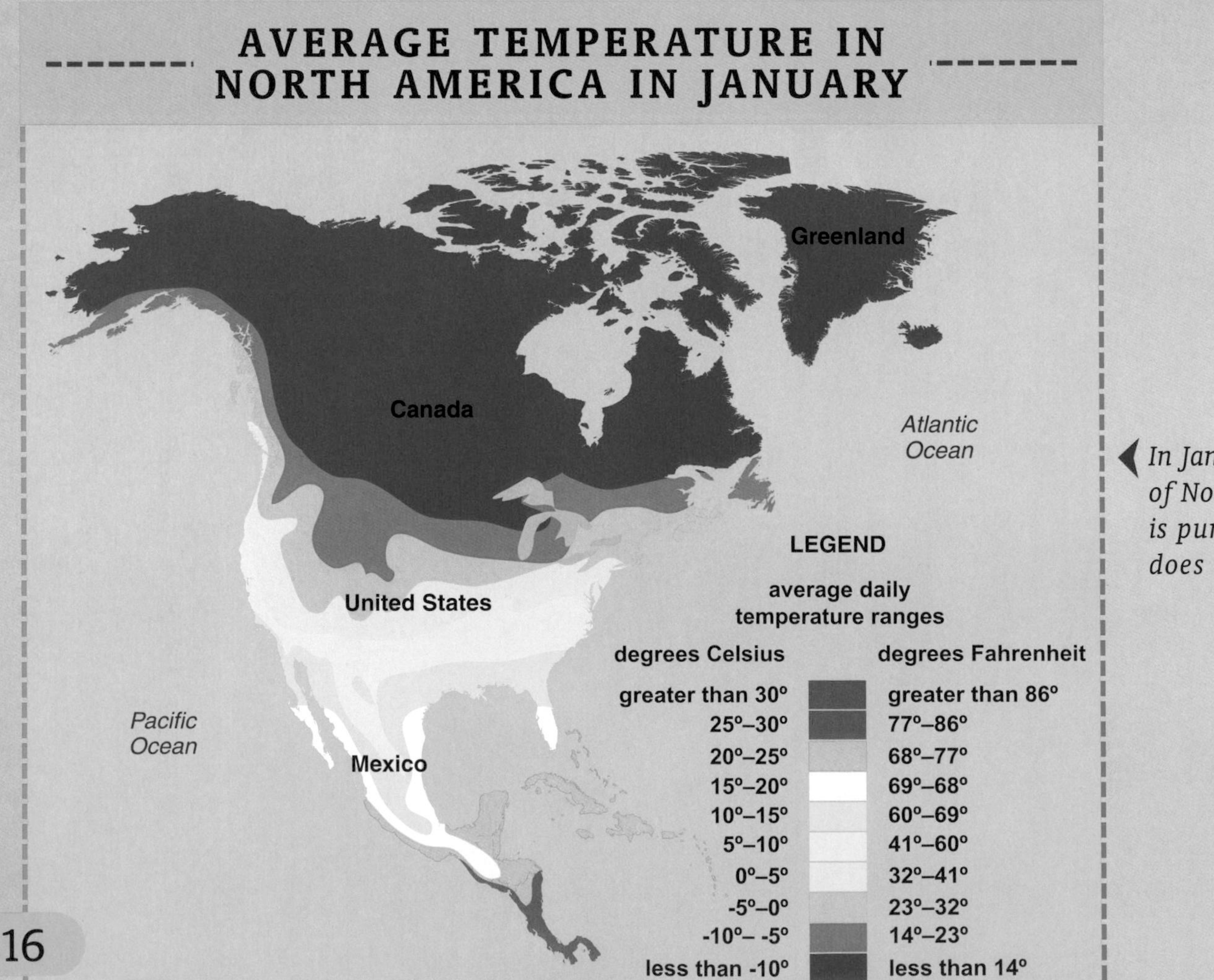

In January, most of North America is purple. What does this mean?

These maps use colors to represent different temperatures. Look at the legend on each map. Which areas have the warmest temperatures in January? Are there any cold places in July?

In July, most of North America heats up. Compare this map with the January map. In which areas do you notice a big increase in temperature? Are there areas where the temperature has only changed slightly?

AVERAGE TEMPERATURE IN NORTH AMERICA IN JULY

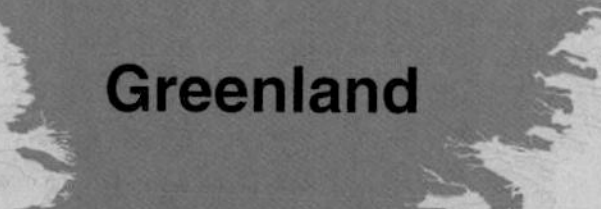

Precipitation Maps

Precipitation maps show how much rain or snow falls over a certain period of time. The map below shows how much precipitation falls in different parts of North America in one year. The colors used on the map and in the legend represent measurements.

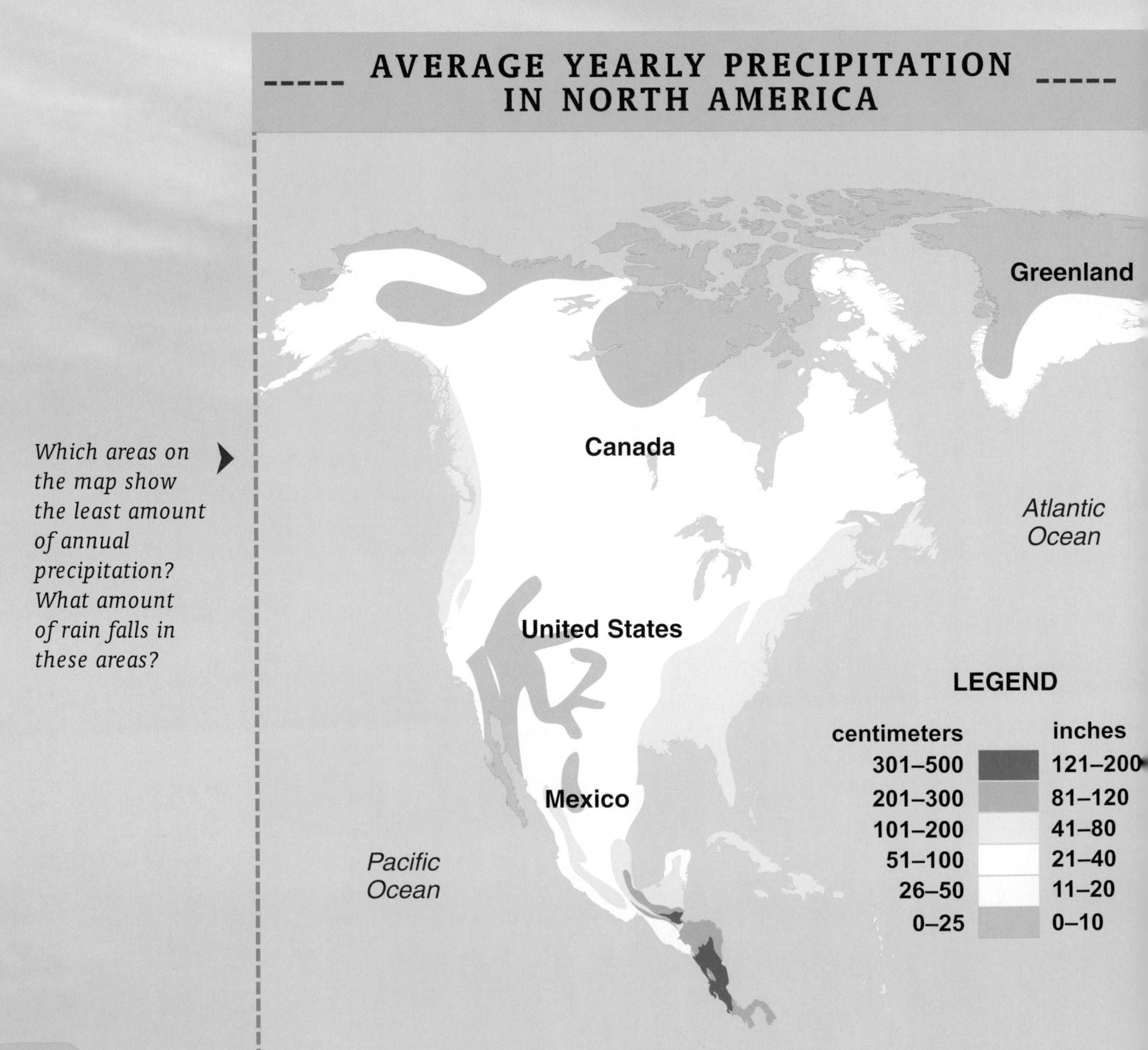

Which areas on the map show the least amount of annual precipitation? What amount of rain falls in these areas?

Each color represents a **range** of the annual precipitation in North America. By looking at the range, you know that the amount of precipitation that fell in an area was no more than the high number and no less then the low number. This lets you know which areas got the most precipitation.

All precipitation begins as ice in the sky. It can change depending on the temperature as it falls. If the air is warmer, it will turn into rain. However, if it is a cold day, it will stay frozen and fall down as snow. What kind of precipitation is most common where you live?

People can measure the amount of snow that falls with a ruler.

Wind Maps

Strong winds affect climate. Wind moves air from one area to another. Air can be warm or cool, and also dry or wet. Winds blow at different speeds. They also go in different directions. Wind maps show us how the air moves around the world.

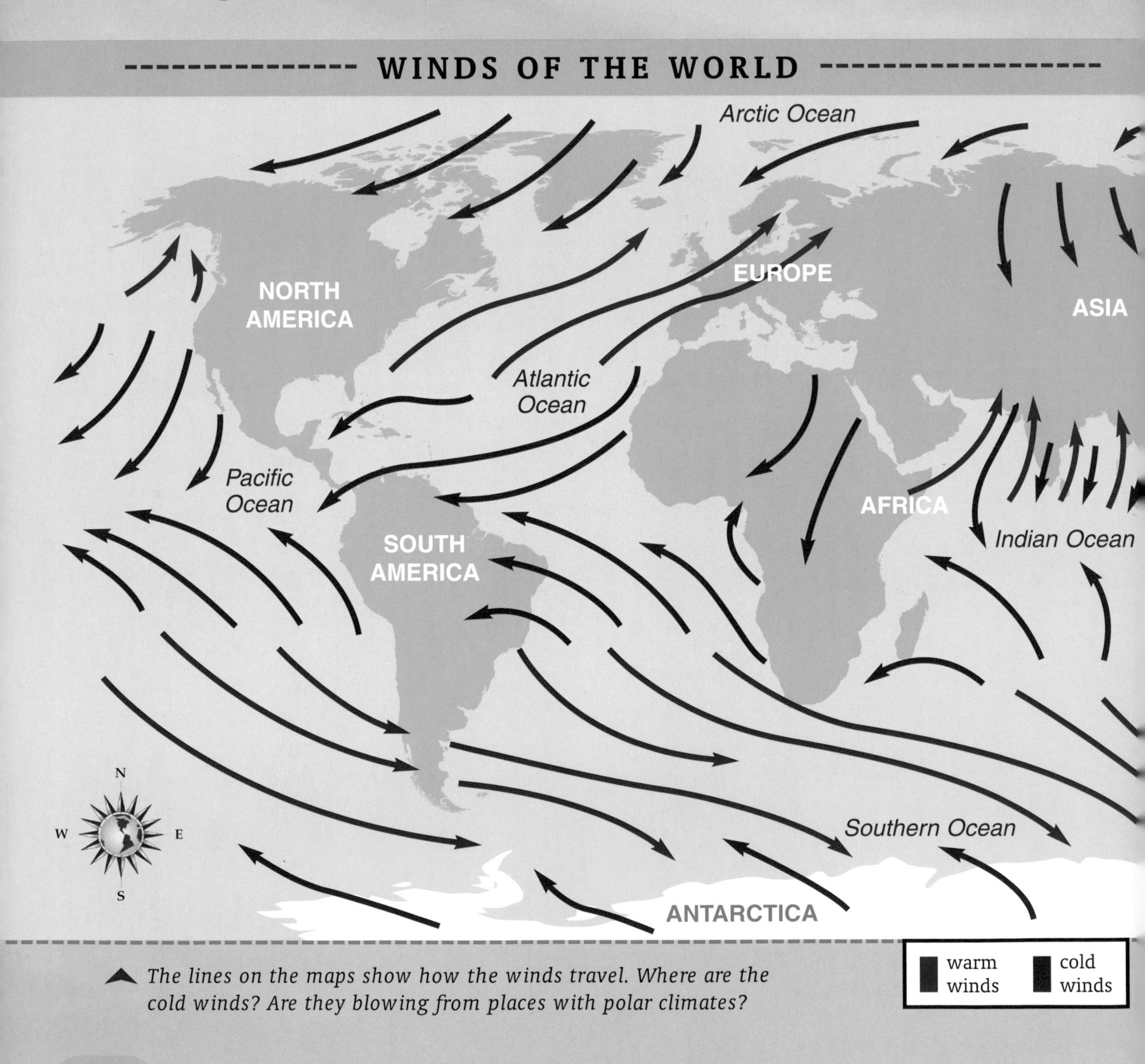

▲ *The lines on the maps show how the winds travel. Where are the cold winds? Are they blowing from places with polar climates?*

Map Facts

Winds that blow across the world have names. *Trade winds* are warm breezes. They blow toward the equator. *Easterlies* blow from east to west. They blow away from the **poles**. *Westerlies* move from west to east. They blow toward the poles. These winds affect the climate in the United States and Canada.

Pacific Ocean

AUSTRALIA/ OCEANIA

In winter, we need a scarf or hat to protect us from a cold wind. In summer, wind cools us down on a hot day. When air moves around, it changes the temperature.

Sometimes the shape of the land gets in the way of the wind. Sometimes it helps the wind move quicker. Winds can travel quickly over flat land, such as the desert. Tall mountains block or slow down the wind.

Strong winds in the desert make ripples in the sand.

Ocean Currents

The wind and the oceans work together. An ocean climate map shows cold and warm ocean **currents**. Cold ocean currents make the air cooler. Land near the cold currents can be dry. Warm ocean currents make the air warmer. This warm air picks up water. Can you guess what happens next? It makes the weather rainy! It usually rains a lot in areas near warm currents.

Follow the ocean current with your finger. It is a pattern. The cold currents turn warm. The warm currents turn cold.

CURRENTS OF THE WORLD

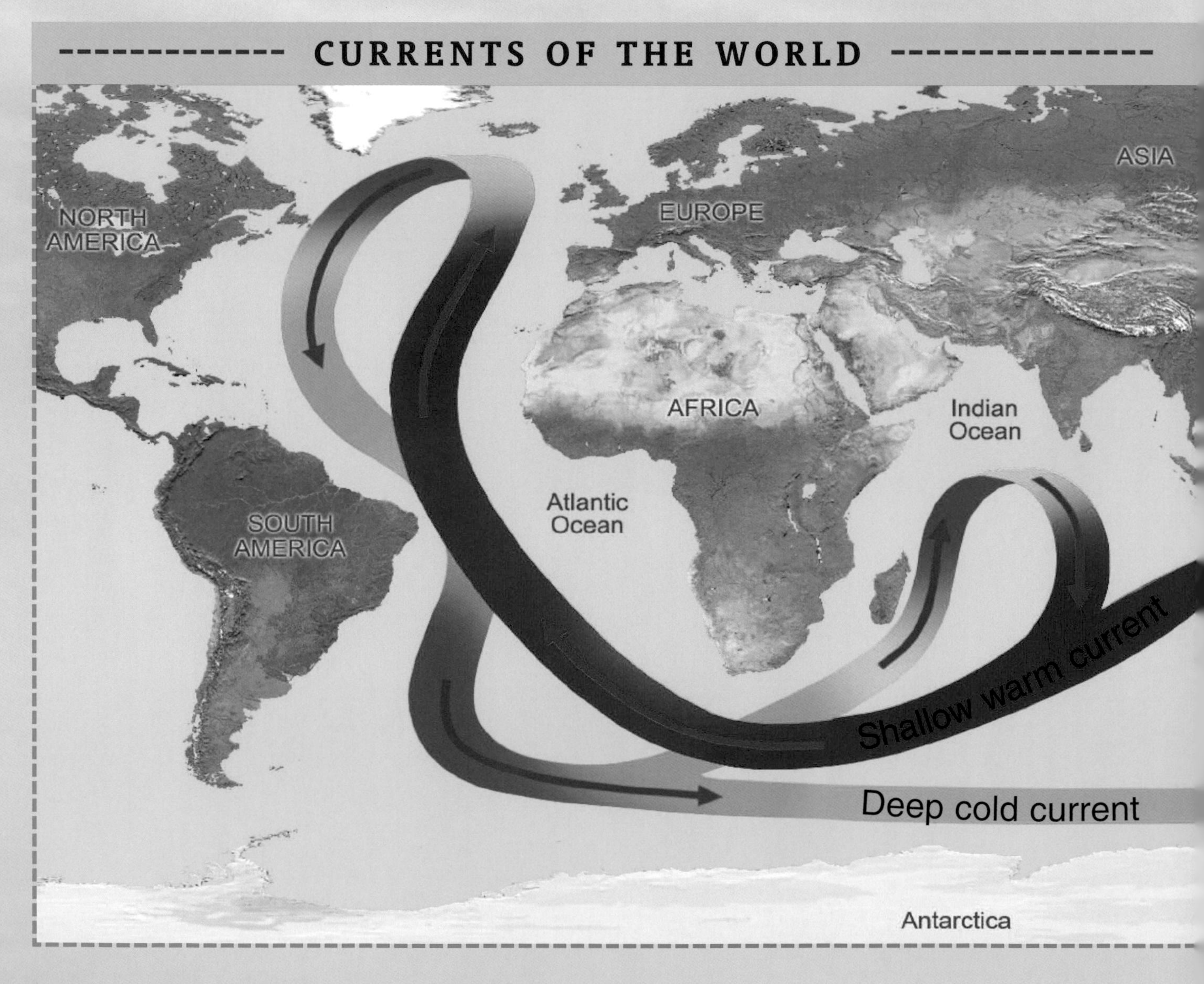

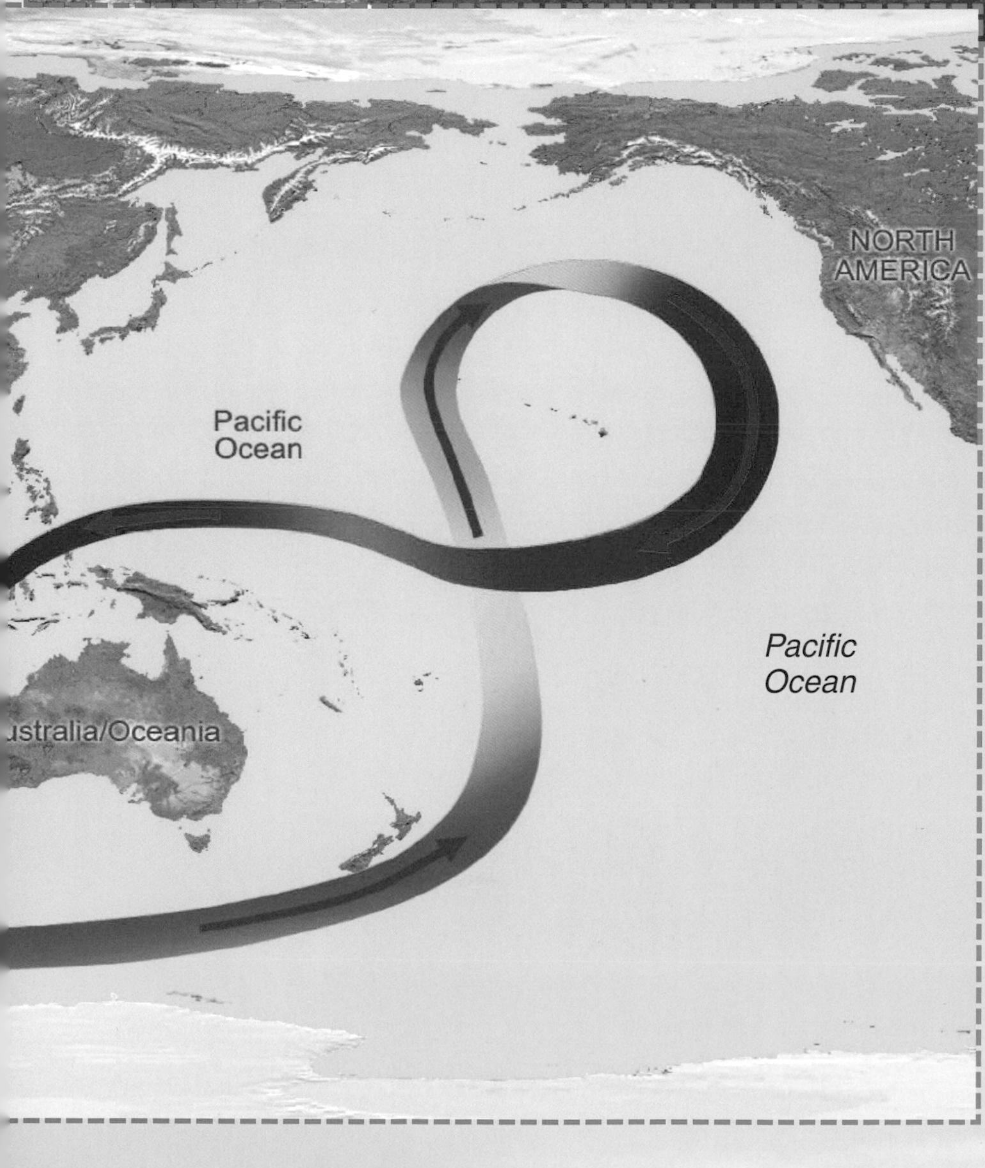

The air picks up water from the ocean and forms clouds.

Ocean currents move around the world. They take warm water to the cold places. They also take cold water to the warmer places. Look at the map to the left to see how this works. What **continent** is close to a big cold current?

El Niño

Most of the time, oceans and winds move in the same direction. Every few years, however, the oceans and winds reverse their direction. This change in the pattern is called El Niño. This shift makes a huge difference to climate. The warm water and wet air move east. Wet places become dry. Usually, El Niño happens in December. It may last for a few weeks or for many months.

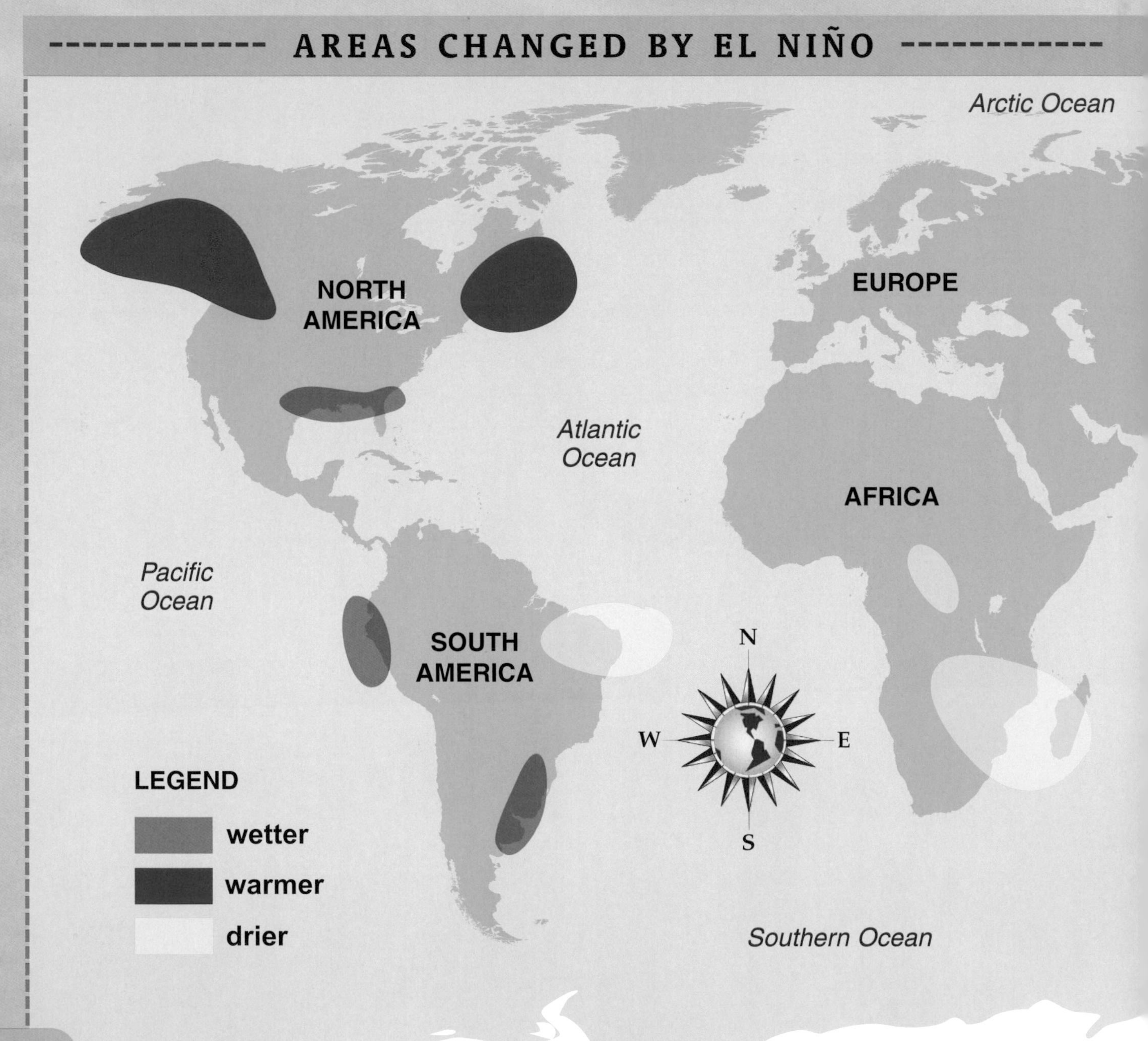

Cold currents bring tiny fish to the surface of the water. Some kinds of penguins eat these fish. When El Niño warms the water, food is hard to find.

ASIA

Pacific Ocean

AUSTRALIA/ OCEANIA

This map shows how El Niño changes the climate in different areas. Scientists study each El Niño to try to understand them.

During El Niño, the normal climate map changes. The areas affected by El Niño are shown on the map to the left. Where in the world do you live? Would El Niño have an effect on you? Which parts of the world are drier than usual? Which parts are warmer?

Extreme Weather

The climate of an area stays the same most of the time. But sometimes, unexpected extreme weather happens. Many kinds of extreme weather occur in warm or tropical climates.

Climate maps can show us where storms often happen.

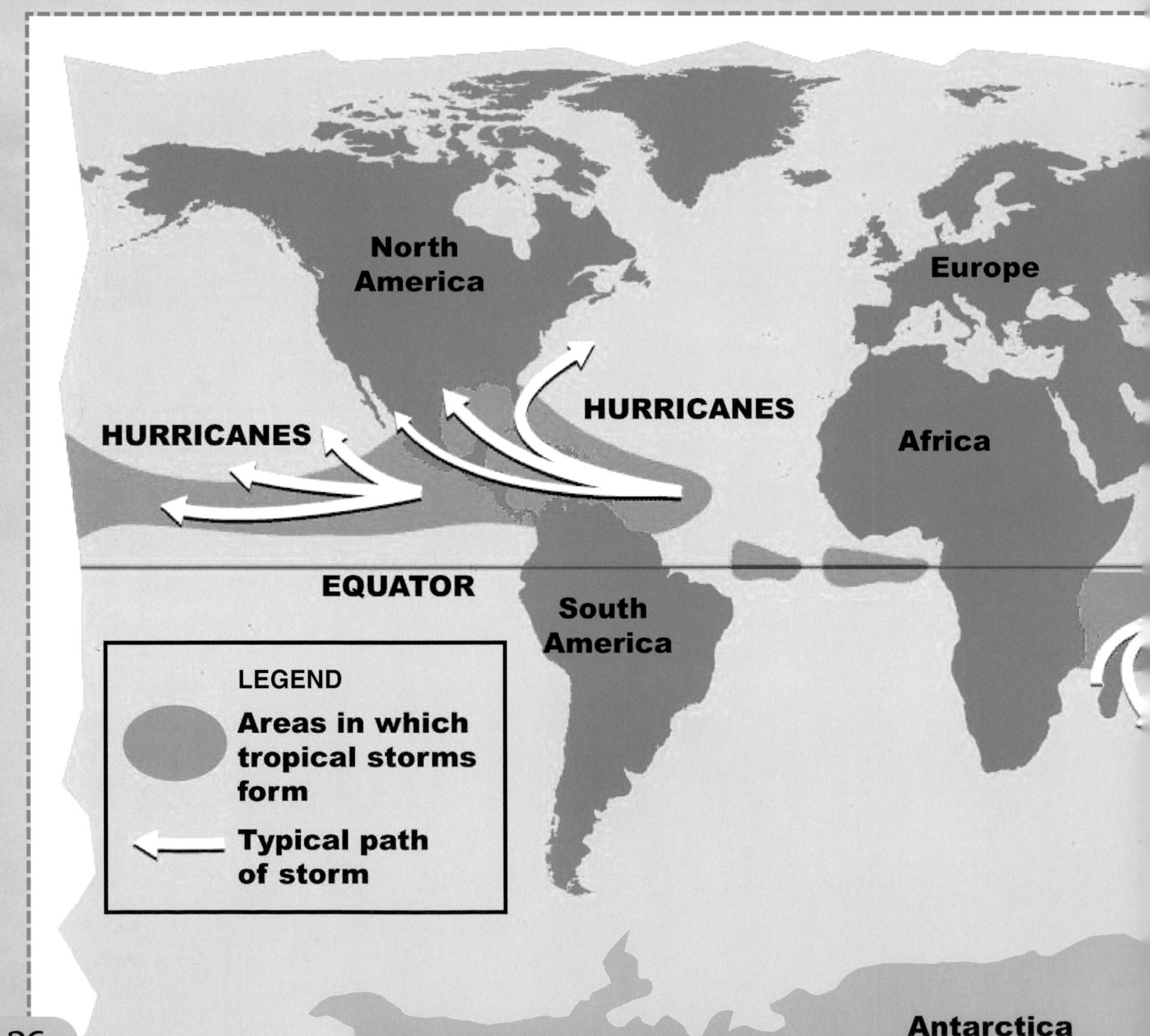

Droughts happen when the land becomes very dry. Too much rain causes floods. Strong winds blow and heavy rains fall during a **hurricane**. A cyclone or typhoon are other names for this kind of storm. Hurricanes form over water. When they move across land, they can cause a lot of damage.

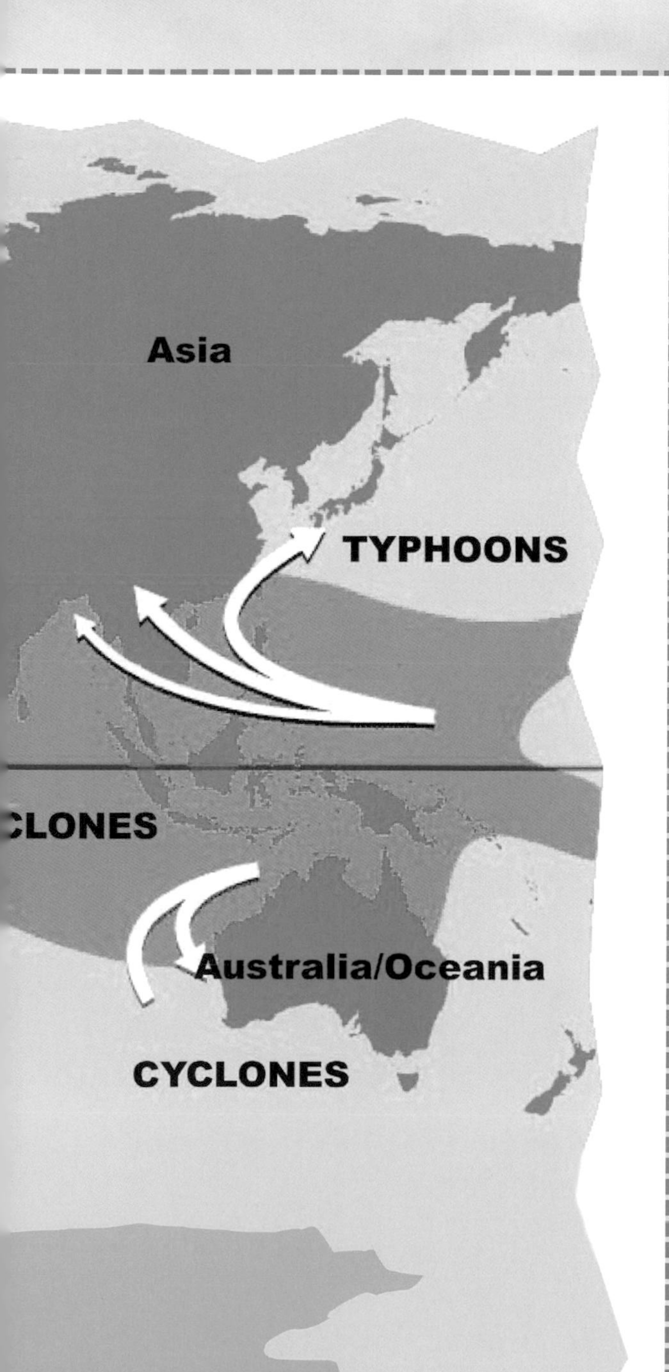

During some kinds of extreme weather, too much water falls at once. Rivers and lakes overflow. What happens to the land?

A climate map can show where these storms form and the direction they are moving. Look at the map on the left. Did you notice that the areas where hurricanes, cyclones, or typhoons form are all close to the equator? Why do you think this is?

Mapping Climate Change

The world's climate is changing. Some parts of the world are getting warmer. Scientists believe this is due to **air pollution**. Even the smallest temperature change can create big problems in an area. Climate maps show us where these changes happen. They can show which places are changing the most.

A WARMING WORLD

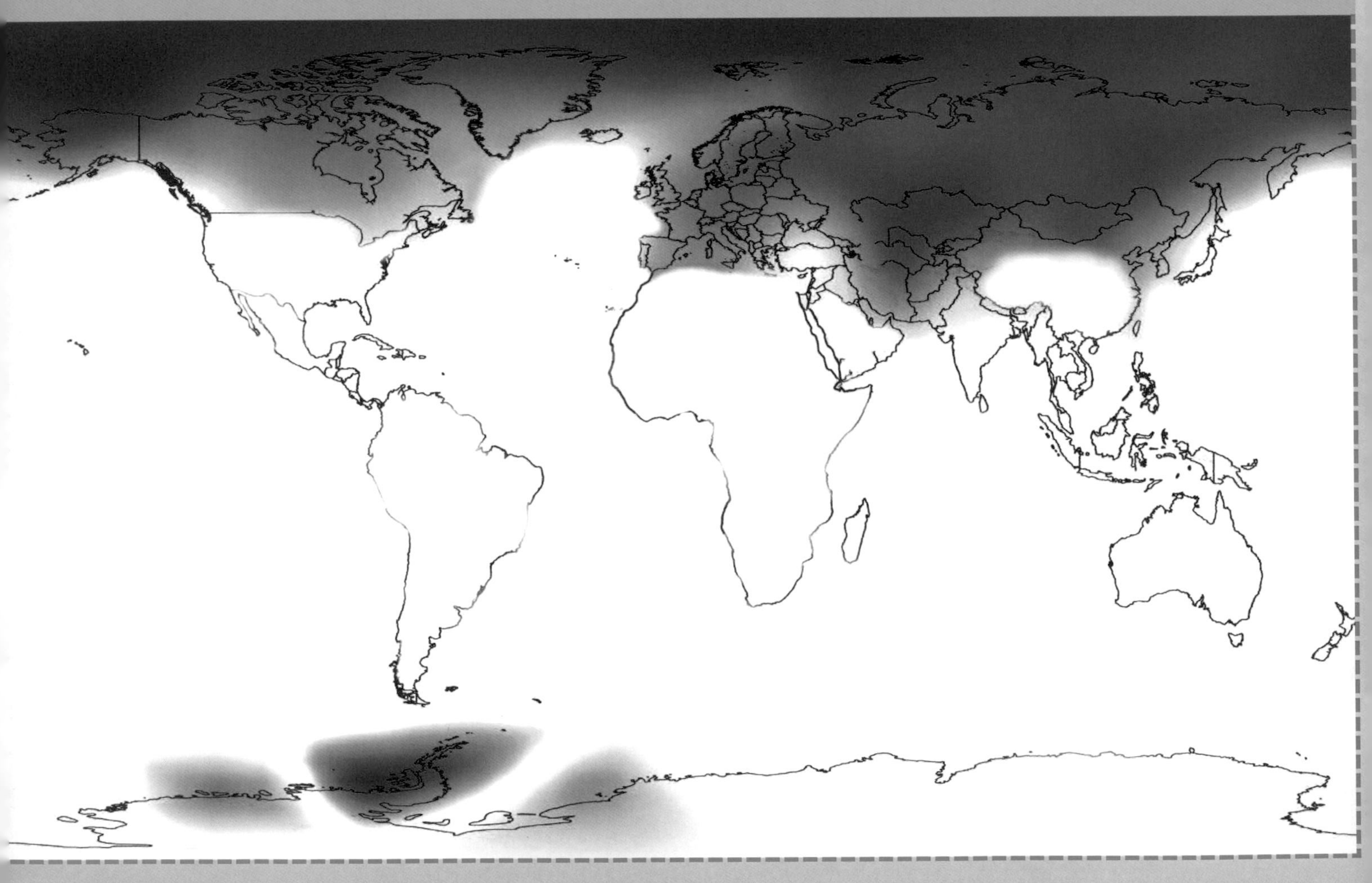

This climate map shows how much of the world is warming up. Dark red means these areas are getting much warmer. Only a small area, marked in blue, has become cooler. Do you think people should be worried about climate change?

Climate changes can have a negative affect on animals living in a certain area. For example, the ice is melting at the poles because of warmer temperatures. Polar bears hunt for seals on the ice. Without the ice to hunt from, it is harder for polar bears to find food.

Scientists use climate information to see which places need our help. They also study climate maps to see if climate change is slowing down. This is important information needed for protecting animals all over the world.

Polar bears live in the Arctic, which is near the North Pole. This part of the world is warming up the most.

Come to my climate!

People often consider climate and weather when choosing a place to visit on vacation. How would you describe the climate and weather where you live to a person who is planning to come there on vacation?

Create a travel brochure to encourage people to visit your city or town. Your brochure should include:

- a description of the climate and weather throughout the year, including information about temperature, wind, and precipitation
- a list of clothing and items to pack for different times of the year (sunglasses, warm sweaters, bathing suits, umbrella, etc.)
- information about the kinds of outdoor activities a person can enjoy. For example, is it warm enough to go swimming in October? Can a visitor go skiing in January?

Include pictures in your brochure.

You can use the internet to look at examples of travel brochures from around the world.

Extension Activity:

Visit the websites below to learn about the climate in different places around the world. Choose a place you would like to visit. Plan an imaginary trip using what you have learned about the climate and weather in that area.

Websites:

This website shows a map of the world's climate zones and describes each climate and its characteristics.

www.kbears.com/climates.html

This website includes temperature and precipitation information for many places around the world.

www.weather-and-climate.com

This website provides links to websites about climate zones, biomes, and weather around the world.

www.nationalgeographic.com/kids-world-atlas/resources.html

This website provides information about the world's climate zones and some facts about climate.

www.blueplanetbiomes.org/climate.htm

To help you decide where to plan your trip, make a list of activities you like to do.

Glossary

Note: Some boldfaced words are defined where they appear in the book.

air pollution Harmful chemicals in the atmosphere

average A usual or expected amount of something

axis A straight line on which an object turns or seems to turn

climate zones Areas with their own type of climate

continent One of the seven main landmasses on Earth

crops Plants that are grown for food, such as soybeans and wheat

currents Bodies of water or air moving in a specific direction

drought A period of time with little or no rain

equator An imaginary line that goes around the middle of Earth

horizontal Going from side to side

hurricane A storm involving very strong winds

legend A map feature that explains the symbols or colors on a map

microclimate The climate of a specific place that is different from the climate in the surrounding areas

poles Extreme north or south point of Earth's axis

range The difference between the greatest number and the least number in a set of data

symbols Pictures that stand for something else

weather station A place designed for recording and reporting observations of the weather in a certain area

Index